One Day at the Time

One Day at the Time

Juhana Day

© 2017 Päivä, Juhana
Kustantaja: BoD – Books on Demand, Helsinki, Suomi
Valmistaja: BoD – Books on Demand, Norderstedt, Saksa
ISBN: 978-951-568-178-2

First Lessons

Beginning

Sun is shining, birds are singing.
I'm sorry, but not my beginning.
snow falling, wind blowing,
awakening into Tuesday morning.
Ten fingers, ten toes,
a million questions, like others, who knows.

First smile in embrace of love,
first chapter, in the part of the heart.
So small and soon ready to walk,
a way that's shown, but a path of its own.

Questions answered, left with one.
Is there a million more, or none.

Pieces

Enjoy life.

But first, there is more to it.

Little by little, and you'll get pieces to fit.

Whenever it's warm you want something to chill,

when it's cold you want some heat, better not get ill.

Make a lot of friends and mostly find only enemies.

You'll see your path, often turning few times your back.

Feel a little joy, to earn more sorrow.

Memories you know, they fill up that hollow.

Getting up. After all,

you've now fallen many times before.

Feel a little blue,

suddenly someone smiles back to you :).

You really can't know that big piece, called Love.

Unless you break this small piece, your heart.

Chained

Time goes by, without slowing or telling you why.

Thing, that's only chained by your mind.

Mind flows around, never silent or leaving you alone.

Thing, that's only chained by your heart.

Heart. Playground of our soul, judge for our feelings.

Endless space divided in two.

One not to keep and one for you.

Bears so much, even more than red and blue.

This thing is not, chained by you.

Best Things

Best things in life,
are often ones that we don't see or value.
until we lose them.

Things that made you smile,
or those that made you cry.
Sweet memories together,
and best friends forever.

Always there,
someone that listened,
even in your despair.

Things that's not easy to find,
never knowing until you've tried.
Some have the power to see these things in life.
Those some, never again,
lose a friend.

Stronger

What is hell to other, only stings a little another.
Show everything, with all your colors.
Keeping the beast inside,
locked, into black and white.

Show no pity, no tears, no pain.
Still feeling them, all the same.
Show your face and the sun will burn,
stay in the shadows and different life you will learn.

What made you fall, now holds you up?
Fear or danger can't hurt you enough.
Shadows see everything like they are,
light couldn't ever take you so far.

Behind your smile it can hurt so much,
no need for showing things that you're not.

Hear the whispers and thoughts in the words,
using it wisely and only to learn.
Though being yourself, opened no doors,
still in others you see all the floors.

Thankful Man

Once I was little, smaller than the rest.
An easy target and put to the test.

Either I looked funny or said the wrong things.
Got hard time, cruelty, you can't believe,
on a daily basis, no relief.

Nature had its play on me,
slowed things down, to put me on ground.

As the time went by, only took one summer,
miracle of my own, I was bigger I was stronger.

Not a soul since crossed my path,
to hit me down, to make me mad.

Little did I know that it changed me forever.

Made me what I am,
a humble, thankful man.

Betrayal

Not To Own

All I have, is yours to hold, yours alone,
but not yours to own.
Something real, something true,
from my heart, for you.

Keep it on your palm, and it will fly away.
Take it in your heart, yours forever, to stay.
Open your door and show me the way,
what else is there, for me to pray.
Because on my own, I will burn my heart,
hoping our love would never apart.

I close my eyes and wait, love should not hesitate.
Something holds so tight. There's no wrong,
when it feels right.

Deception

Winter cold won't ease that burn,
when course of nature takes it's turn.
Showing to you it's darkest days,
might open your eyes to reveal your cage.

Greater that storm what lies beneath.
One could witness and another has foreseen.

Trying to close your eyes,
but from new tomorrow,
you cannot hide.

Stay Or Go

Should I spread my wings to stay or go...?

Promises made, promises broken.

I know I should go.

I could stay, forgiving lies and pain,

Cruelty and deceive, endless vain.

No. You should go.

For Someone Else

If there's a way for me to be with you,
it wouldn't be in this world, no, it can't be true.

One that knows me, who I am.
Sees beneath me, in just a glance.
One that noticed when I didn't look.
In a smile and a hello, that's all it took.

Had a beginning like all the other,
but have no ending,
like winter or a summer.

Far away or next to me,
her eyes, her voice,
lives in a part of me.

There's no more sorrow, no despair.
Her lies, her choice,
meant for someone else,
you were.

Fading Away

Where is the savior I need the most?
I cannot eat or sleep, I look like a ghost.

All alone in this cold house,
trapped in these walls, like a mouse.
I'm fading away, I cannot lie,
Trying to find a piece of mind.

Then I saw my sister, she broke into tears.
To hurt my closest, one of my greatest fears.

I can't believe, I've been so foolish,
Time to do something, before I perish.

Venom

Cursed by a venomous heart.

Forget, but it never gives up.

Regret, but it's not going to stop.

Admit, your torment gets tighten.

Forgive,

and your burden is lighten.

From The Ashes

Something To Miss

Once loved, or what it seemed.
Loved once and so, opened the deep.

Never knew it could be so easy,
never saw it before it hit me.

Where no dream or fantasy could ever exceed,
when power of will is getting on its knees.

One feeling never dies,
but burns to show you this.

Always there to remind,
how much can you miss.

Tomorrow

Tomorrow... So often heard
At the end of the day, it's only a word.

Today, can be found in a mirror.
Eye to eye your destiny,
say hello to your friend,
your dearest enemy.

Might see more than the image that would not last,
or shadowed reflections of the past

Those of whom that wish to suffer,
in every moment there's no more,
than tomorrow.

Faith For Fate

You can't fight fate,
especially the one that you made.

Find places unknown, all alone.
Faith in a key for happiness,
or locked in the truth of sadness.

Learn it, like in a game.
Every love,
there's a lesson for pain.

Greatest Gift

Dry your tears of sorrow,
they stain your face so beautiful.
Never meant so from the start,
there's a reason why it feels so hard.

Who would change you,
break you, no one could.
You're meant for something more.

Don't question who you are,
what you become or what you do.
Time shows everything,
now preparing, wanting just you.

Don't wait, it won't warn or hesitate.
Eyes shut and holding your ears,
your heart, your fears.

Can't write about it,
not a feeling to chain by words.
For others brings that greatest gift,
those few who values, all of it.

Guardian Angel

Angel with tears.
Heart, full of fears.
Wings without feathers.
No more to tear, for others.

Angel with eyes dark,
now sees through the light and shadows.

Knows no meaning for its existence,
through the past and the time that follows.

Waiting answers from above or below,
still awake and learning, from sorrow.

But when there is life there is laughter,
a little smile or kindness from the other.

Always holding burnt heart and a scar,
this angel will never, take the side of the dark.

Past

My abyss, my history,
for many, uncharted territory.

You should leave it all behind,
already written and endured.
Mind is aware, never blind,
so much more to be prepared.

Should you look ahead in the mist,
there you begin, there you exist.

Life and its divine glory,
well that's another,
untold story.

Feed The Pain

Bounds

One beautiful morning, after the rain,
felt like, I was hit by a train.

Fiery spikes, chained to my throne,
the grip gets tighter, the cause unknown.

Like something tearing you from your spine,
this is the everyday life of mine.

Ankylosing spondylitis,
as poetic as it sounds.
No control over me,
I set the bounds.

Legacy

Same things we are made of.
Still different in gifts we own,
in our flesh, our blood and bone.

It's pouring like a rain,
when it's time to feed the pain.

Burning in agony, injured in this war,
fighter in me, is beginning to roar.

Sleepless nights, dusk till dawn,
survivor in me, has been born.

No one's prophecy
this one is mine.
My legacy.

Gift

Pain is not a stranger to me.

It's a teacher, companion and a reminder at least.

Teacher of stamina and humility,

Reminding of life that was granted to me.

Trying to be a good boy,

so I'll do my best to enjoy,

this gift, this pain,

we so want to avoid.

Words

It hurts so bad you can't describe.

Hurt by the words you build up inside.

The pen is truly a sword of a kind,

leaves wounds and scars not to be seen by eyes.

Still the words left unsaid,

are crucial and worthy instead.

Defeat

Nobody's perfect, but always try,

reach the stars, highest in the sky.

Defeat means nothing unless you quit.

When you lose everything,

you have everything to give.

Pursue your dreams and endure life.

Sometimes it means, one day at a time.

Old Friend

Woke up this morning, something is wrong.
My heart, its mad, it's out of control!
Feel like it's ticking,
ticking like a bomb.

Old friend called Fear came along,
hit me like a spear, I thought it was gone.

Soon on my way, under the knife,
thinking, this might be my last fight.

I was awake when it stopped, no beat,
no rhythm, everything locked.

Seconds it took, felt like eternity,
my life, it was given, back to me.

Something stayed on that table however,
old friend called Fear,
left me forever.

You And Me

Eyes

What do you see, are you looking at all?
Hunger of a beast, wanting you to fall.
Claws of danger to feast with your heart,
just waiting to tear you apart.

Or a soul and a mind of a lonely ranger,
depth in the eyes, different kind of a creature.
Some are not born wild in nature.

Sometimes eyes only show,
what heart fears the most.

Shield

Hello there.
Can you see me?
Oh, you can.

You're not running away I see.
Broke right through my shield of steel.

My body starts to tremble inside,
many have fallen, many have tried.

A lion was set on its path tonight,
yet kitten took over and leaned by your side.

You bring out the best in me.
In your arms, beast in the deep,
found its shelter and is now asleep.

Home

At last I hear more than silence,
finally I see more than darkness.

Last breath of ice, the first of fire,
casts a light on the shadow of desire.

Feel a heartbeat start,
you are holding my heart.

Hard as a stone, it had its shell.
Now all exposed, under your spell.

I'm not alone...
I'm home.

Beside Me

Next to you, hand on your cheek,
feel your warmth on my skin.
Nowhere else I rather be,
beside you so much more I feel.

The power that binds and holds us together,
no law of physics or power can measure.

Letter for you I wanted to write,
never have I found, such love and its might.

This is where I choose to be,
If you're there,
beside me.

Never Far

It took a while,

but our paths crossed.

I was a wanderer, everything lost,

by your side whatever the cost.

I love everything that you are.

In my sky, you're the brightest star.

In my heart, you're never far.

Man's Job

To stand by her, in storm and thunder,

to make a winter to feel like a summer.

To dry the tears in her eyes,

to catch the spider and all kinds of flies.

To uphold her dreams, her love and faith,

to succeed where others have failed.

This is what a man is for,

a man's job is all that and more.

Silent Lullaby

Void

Our life, our story.
Every morning, we can't avoid
Day after day, this gruesome void.
Something hurting, something missing.
Every day it keeps on reminding.

Night falls in our empty arms
Forcing us to glance at the stars.
We see, thus,
not even one, for us?

Needless to say,
every moment awake,
seeing the stars multiply,
anything that can magnify,
this silent, unsung lullaby.
Hoping that maybe once we see,
that one,
one for you and me.

Judge

Something, somewhere,
You,
up there, anywhere.

For this one time, hear me out.
You do not judge, control or cast me out!
We deserve more than this.
Grant me just one wish,
I must have earned that joy,
that bliss.
May have broken a mirror or few.
Years, more than seven I went through.

Anything more?
I shall do.

In Time

We've been through sadness and joy,
together we encountered our horse of Troy.

Today you told me you carry inside,
a little beginning, a meaning of a life.

Out of words, almost ready to cry.
This chapter has an end,
with a tear of joy and a sigh.

Strength to those in this battle alike,
it could be you, next in line.
Just try to be strong,
all in time.

Pa-pum

Pa-pum, pa-pum...

So faint, so tiny.

So fragile, we treasure so highly.

Yet, fills our dreams so vast,

shed light on our past.

In embrace of a womb,

pa-pum, pa-pum.

One Wish

I had a wish, only one.
To have a daughter, or a son.

Got more wishes not just one...

I wish I can see you growing up.
I wish I can see you fall in love.
I wish I can be close,
when you need me the most.
I wish you will know, I love you so.

I wish I'll be there all the way.
If I'm not, at least I can say,
I got one wish,
sealed with a kiss.

All You Need

Will you have
the beauty of your mother,
or strength of your father.

My eyes, my passion.
Her smile, her spirit and
infinite compassion.

What will you be,
we just need to wait and see.

What is for sure,
you will have all that you need,
and more.

Out Of Time

Castaway

I remember it like yesterday,
everything was black and grey.
Thoughts and feelings of a castaway.

On a journey that had no end,
all the colors began to blend.
Not all just darkness did I see,
little glints of light surrounded me.

At the end I was the one,
with the power, to turn it around.
If I'd known what I know now,
I wouldn't have bow down.

Forever

Life is short they say.
You only believe what you see, ok.

Never wondered why things go the way they do?
Laws set, not by a man, not like me and you.
Always thinking what's right, what's wrong,
why so fast or why it's taking so long.

Here to learn or to pay the price,
for this voyage of the soul,
soul of a thousand lives.

Seeing so much, or leaving it all behind,
New beginning, under the moon or the sunlight.

Restless souls, young at heart.
They'll never get old, here forever.
One story, told.

Silent Words

Seen it happen, seen it fall,

reign of terror on us all.

Aftermath of silence, everybody hurts.

Wisdom speaks so silent words.

Aren't we learned a lesson or two.

Time to listen and follow through,

statement of the heart,

in me and you.

Fortune

There's an end for everything,

so is told.

But not for some,

be brave, be bold.

Era of love, not for war.

An eternity, unseen before.

Awaken hunger,

hunger for more.

Within our hearts, in yours and mine.

Fortune that is not,

bound by time.

When

When I leave without saying goodbye.
When it rains, I can see your tears, you feel mine.

When you're asleep,
could you hear a whisper in your ear?
When you speak to me, I'm not far but very near.

When you're alone,
would you feel when I'm coming close?
When it gets cold, can you feel a little kiss to your nose?